World War II
Cumulative Index

World War II
Cumulative Index

Includes Indexes For:

World War II: Almanac
World War II: Biographies
World War II: Primary Sources

Christine Slovey, Index Coordinator

AN IMPRINT OF THE GALE GROUP

DETROIT · SAN FRANCISCO · LONDON
BOSTON · WOODBRIDGE, CT

Christine Slovey, *Index Coordinator*

Printed in the United States of America

10 9 8 7 6 5

Cumulative Index

A = World War II: Almanac
B = World War II: Biographies
P = World War II: Primary Sources

A

Aachen, Germany
  A *2:* 302 (ill.)
Abbey, at Monte Cassino
  A *2:* 237, 238 (ill.), 239 (ill.)
Abwehr (German military
  counter-intelligence)
  A *2:* 350
Action in the North Atlantic
  A *2:* 384–85
Advisory Council for Italy
  A *2:* 220
Africa (*See* North Africa)
African Americans
  A *1:* 112–19
African Americans, and armed
  services
  A *1:* 114–17, 114 (ill.), 116 (ill.)
  B 43, 46–49, 51, 57, 58, 116
African Americans, and defense
  industry jobs
  A *1:* 113
African Americans, and migration
  from south
  A *1:* 108, 118

Afrika Korps
  A *1:* 70–71, *2:* 227
  B 157, 162, 163, 208, 223, 226,
  228, 241
Air force, Allied
  A *1:* 55–60, 57 (ill.), *2:* 253–54,
  263–64
Air raids
  A *1:* 182–93
Air raids, against Britain
  A *1:* 55–60, 58 (ill.), 59 (ill.),
  185–86, 185 (ill.)
Air raids, against Germany
  A *1:* 188–93
Air raids, against Japan
  A *1:* 101, 334–35
Air raids, British civilians killed by
  A *1:* 59
Air raids, German civilians
  wounded by
  A *2:* 394
Air raids, the Doolittle raid
  A *1:* 101
Air Transport Authority (ATA)
  B 38

Boldface type indicates
abbreviation of individual titles;

Bold numerals indicate
main entries

Illustrations are marked by (ill.).

Airborne troops
  A *2:* 263–64
Aircraft industry
  A (U.S.) *1:* 106–07, 120
AK (*Armia Krajowa*) (*See* Home
    Army [Polish])
Alamein, El
  A *2:* 228
Albania
  A *1:* 72–73
Albrecht, Berty
  B 70
Aleutians
  A *2:* 316–17
Algeria
  A *2:* 228–30
Alliance
  A *2:* 354
Allies
  A *2:* 205–19
  B 151–53, 174–75, 209, 211,
    228, 240–43, 252
  P 6, 22, 45, 47, 66, 81, 119,
    123, 125, 129, 130, 138, 140,
    143, 144, 156, 173–75, 184,
    187, 193, 205, 211, 212, 220
Ambrose, Stephen E.
  P 187–96
American Civil Liberties Union
    (ACLU)
  B 131
Anglo-American Control
    Commission (Italy)
  A *2:* 220
Anschloss
  A *1:* 20 (ill.), 21
  B 123
Anti-Comintern Pact (1936)
  A *1:* 32, 83
Anti-Communism
  A *2:* 371
Anti-Semitism
  A *1:* 2, 157–68, 375–76, 381
  B 84, 102, 105, 108, 109, 201,
    259, 260, 267
  P 35, 101, 102
Anti-Semitism, and motion
    pictures
  A *2:* 375–76
Antwerp
  P187
Anzio, Italy
  A *2:* 237–38
  B 49

Appeasement
  A *1:* 21–22
  B 13, 28
  P 5, 15
Arcadia Conference
  A *2:* 208–09
Ardennes Forest
  A *1:* 48–49, 49 (ill.) *2:* 292
Ardennes offensive (*See* Battle
    of the Bulge)
Area bombing
  A *1:* 188–89, 193
Arizona, *USS*
  A *1:* 90, 92, 92 (ill.), 118
  P 60 (ill.), 61, 67
Armia Krajowa (AK) (*See* Home
    Army [Polish])
Armistice, French-German (1940)
  A *1:* 54
Armistice, World War I
  A *1:* 4
Army Group Center (German)
  A *1:* 81–82, *2:* 279–80
Army Group North (German)
  A *1:* 81
Army Nurse Corps (ANC)
  P 159, 168, 169
The Army of the Future
  B 64
Arnold, General A.H. "Hap"
  B 38
Arsenal of Democracy
  A *1:* 63, 106
Asia for the Asians policy
  A *1:* 31, *2:* 414
Athenia
  P 43, 44 (ill.)
Athens
  A *1:* 74 (ill.), 75–76, 136
Atlantic, Battle of (*See* Battle of
    the Atlantic)
Atlantic Charter
  A *2:* 208, 414
  B 240
  P 22, 23, **26–27**, 29
Atlantic Wall
  A *2:* 254–55, 255 (ill.), 353
Atomic bomb
  A *2:* 223, 337–44, 338 (ill.), 340
    (ill.), 363–68
  B 97, 143, 183, 185, 189, 190,
    241, 275, 278, 281–83
  P 117–28, 121 (ill.), 129–42, 213

Atomic Energy Commission
  B 191–92
Atrocities
  A 1: 30, 32, 157–79, 2: 218–19,
    298–99,
Attu
  A 2: 316
Auschwitz
  A 1: 178–79, 178 (ill.) 202,
    2: 297
  B 256, 260
  P 108, 109, 111, 112
Australia
  A 1: 61, 101–02, 2: 312, 393
Australian troops
  A 2: 318–19
Austria
  A 1: 4, 21, 160, 162, 2: 403
Axis
  A 1: 69, 72, 75 (ill.), 103,
    2: 205, 224–26
  B 109, 167, 172
  P 6, 60, 61, 67, 87, 143
Axis Sally (Mildred Gillars)
  A 2: 372

B

Babi Yar
  A 1: 171
Baby boom
  A 2: 406
Badoglio, Pietro
  A 2: 235
  P 213
Bagration, Operation
  A 2: 278–82
Barbarossa, Operation
  A 1: 77–82, 79 (ill.)
Bari, Italy
  A 1: 195
Barker, Rodney
  P 129–42
Bastogne, Belgium
  P 193
Bataan
  A 1: 96–97, 2: 327
  P 65
Bataan Death March
  A 1: 97
Battle of Britain
  A 1: 55–60, 58 (ill.), 59 (ill.),
    182 (ill.), 185–86, 2: 201
    (ill.), 360

Battle of Dunkirk (See Dunkirk)
Battle of El Alamein (See El
    Alamein)
Battle of Iwo Jima (See Iwo Jima)
Battle of Kursk (See Kursk)
Battle of Midway
  A 1: 102–03, 2: 357
  P 65, 66
Battle of Okinawa (See Okinawa)
Battle of Stalingrad
  A 2: 244–46, 246 (ill.)
  P 37, 39
Battle of the Atlantic
  A 1: 66–69, 68 (ill.), 2: 227
  P 43–58, 54 (ill.)
Battle of the Bulge
  A 2: 292 (ill.), 292–94
  B 78, 165, 200
  P 187–96, 189 (ill.), 190 (ill.),
    191 (ill.), 193 (ill.), 195 (ill.)
Battle of the Bulge, and African-
    American troops
  A 1: 115
Battle of the Bulge, and
    intelligence
  A 2: 346
Battle of the Coral Sea
  A 1: 100 (ill.), 101–02
BBC (See British Broadcasting
    Corporation)
"Be Ye Men of Valour"
  P 11–13
Beethoven's Fifth Symphony
  A 2: 371
Belarus (See White Russia)
Belgium
  A 1: 47–48, 49 (ill.), 138, 183,
    2: 270, 355, 396
Belorussia (See White Russia)
Belzec concentration camp
  A 1: 173
Bengal, famine in (1943)
  A 2: 412
Benning Revolution
  B 150
Bergman, Ingrid
  A 2: 382, 382 (ill.)
Berlin
  A 1: 191, 2: 395 (ill.), 397 (ill.)
Berlin, Battle of
  A 2: 301–04
Bertin, Celia
  B 70

Bethe, Hans
A *2:* 366
Bielsko, Poland
A *1:* 164
Bismarck
P 48, 49 (ill.)
Black Code (American attaché
code)
A *2:* 357
Black market
A *1:* 110, 112, 136
Black shirts (Italy)
A *1:* 12
B 170
Blackout
A *1:* 187, 200
Bletchley Park (Ultra
headquarters)
A *2:* 358
The Blitz (*See* Battle of Britain)
Blitzkrieg
A *1:* 40–41
B 225, 226
P 8, 188
"Blood, Toil, Tears and Sweat"
B 30
P 10–11
Blücher (German battleship)
A *1:* 47
Blue Max, Hermann Göring
awarded
B 83
Bock's Car
P 138
Bogart, Humphrey
A *2:* 382, 382 (ill.)
Bohec, Jeanne
B 70
Bohemia
A *1:* 23
Bolshevism
B 247, 248
P 38
Bombardment, air, D-Day
A *2:* 264
Bombardment, naval, D-Day
A *2:* 264
Bomber Command (Royal Air
Force)
A *1:* 188–89, 193
"Bomber" Harris (*See* Harris, Sir
Arthur)
Bombing of London
B 206

Bond drives
A *1:* 108
Bonin Islands
A *2:* 326 (ill.)
Bonus March
B 139
Book burnings
A *2:* 373
Bosnia
A *1:* 154–55
Bougainville
A *2:* 318, 357
Bourke-White, Margaret
A *2:* 387
B 266
Boycott, anti-Jewish
A *1:* 159
Bradley, General Omar
B 196, 200
Braun, Eva
A *2:* 303
B 111
Britain (*See* Great Britain)
British Army, and the Battle of
Falaise (Normandy)
A *2:* 269
British Army, evacuation from
Dunkirk
A *1:* 51–53
British Army, in Greece
A *1:* 76
British Army, in invasion of
Normandy
A *2:* 260, 265
British Army, in North Africa
A *1:* 69–72
British Army, women in
A *1:* 197–98
British Broadcasting Corporation
(BBC)
A *1:* 138, *2:* 370
British Expeditionary Force (BEF)
A *1:* 48, 50–53
Broad front strategy
A *2:* 292
Brokaw, Tom
P 87, 95
Brotherhood of Sleeping Car
Porters
A *1:* 112
Brown Shirts (*See* Storm Troopers)
Broz, Josip (*See* Tito)
Brussels, liberation of
A *2:* 270

B-25 bomber
  A *1:* 101
B-29 bomber (superfortress)
  A *2:* 327–28, 334–35
Bukharin, Nikolai
  B 249
Bulgaria
  A *1:* 73–74, *2:* 225–26, 298–99
Bulge, Battle of the (*See* Battle of
    the Bulge)
Burma
  A *1:* 84–85, 99, *2:* 305
Burma Road
  A *1:* 84–85, *2:*306 (ill.)
Bush, George
  P 94
Buzz-bomb (*See* V-1)

C

Caen, France
  A *2:* 260, 268
The Cage
  P 104–12
Cairo Conference
  B 22
Cairo, Egypt
  A *2:* 357
"Call to Honor"
  B 66
Canada
  A *1:* 61
Canada, joint defense planning
    with U.S.
  A *1:* 65
Canadian Army, and D-Day
  A *2:* 260
Canadian Army, and the Battle
    of Falaise (Normandy)
  A *2:* 269
Canadian Army, and the
    Dieppe raid
  A *2:* 257
Canaris, Admiral Wilhelm
  A *2:* 350, 354
Capra, Frank
  A *2:* 379
  B 1–10, 1 (ill.)
Casablanca
  A *2:* 382 (ill.), 382–83
Casablanca Conference
  A *2:* 214 (ill.), 215–16

Casablanca, Morocco
  A *2:* 228, 230
  B 243
  P 221
Cassino
  A *2:* 236–38, 238 (ill.), 239 (ill.)
Casualties
  A *2:* 391–93
Catholicism
  B 259-261
Caucasus
  A *2:* 242, 246
Cavalry (Polish)
  A *1:* 40–41, 41 (ill.)
Censorship
  A *1:* 138, *2:* 376
Chain reaction, nuclear
  A *2:* 364–65
Chamberlain, Neville
  A *1:* 22, 48
  B 11–16, 11 (ill), 14 (ill.), 28
  P 5, 15
Chelmno concentration camp
  A *1:* 173
Chetniks
  A *1:* 153–54
Chiang Kai-Shek
  A *1:* 33, *2:* 222 (ill.)
  B 17–24, 17 (ill), 23 (ill)
Children
  A *1:* 121, 124–25, 199–204, 201
    (ill.), 203 (ill.), *2:* 304 (ill.),
    338 (ill.)
China, and Korea
  A *1:* 28
China, Civil war in
  A *1:* 33
China, Communist Party of
  A *1:* 33
China, establishment of the
    Republic
  A *1:* 33
China, Japanese atrocities in
  A *1:* 30
China, Japanese invasion of
  A *1:* 27–29, 32–34
  B 20, 21
China, Japanese troops in
  A *2:* 305
China, losses in the war
  A *2:* 411
Choltitz, Dietrich von
  A *2:* 273, 275

Chuikov, Vasili
  A *2:* 244
Churchill, Winston
  A *1:* 48, 53, *2:* 207–11, 214 (ill.),
    221 (ill.), 230, 252, 336 (ill.)
  B 13, 25 (ill.), **25–33**, 29 (ill.),
    66, 223, 240, 242 (ill.), 243
  P **5–19**, 9 (ill.), 18 (ill.), **21–30**,
    26 (ill.), 44, 55, 56 (ill.), 78,
    119, 120, 123, 140, 194
Ciano, Galeazzo
  B 174
Citizen Soldiers
  P **188–92**
Civilian Conservation Corps
  B 150
Clark, General Mark
  B 163
Cochran, Jacqueline
  B **34–42**, 34 (ill.), 37 (ill)
Code Talker Alphabet
  B 178
Code Talkers (*See* Navaho
  Code Talkers)
Codes and code-breaking
  A *1:* 66, *2:* 356–59
Cold War
  A *2:* 397
  B 255
Collaboration
  A *1:* 148, 149 (ill.)
Collective security
  A *1:* 6
Cologne, air raid
  A *1:* 189, 190 (ill.)
Colonies
  A *2:* 208, 413
Combined Chiefs of Staff
  A *2:* 209
Commandos
  A *2:* 257, 266
Common Market
  A *2:* 396
Communications
  B 175–79
Communism
  A *1:* 151–52, *2:* 206, 219, 283
  B 6, 19–22, 24, 80, 144, 154,
    185, 192, 245, 246, 248, 249,
    285, 287
  P 38, 39, 123, 219
Communist Party
  A *1:* 7, 16, 17, 33, *2:* 272, 411

Compton, Arthur
  B 190
Concentration camps
  A *1:* 16, 172–76
  B 109, 266, 270
  P 103, 112, 113 (ill.), 114
Confessions of a Nazi Spy
  A *2:* 379
Congressional Medal of Honor,
  James Doolittle awarded
  B 274
Conscientious objection
  B 121, 123–27
Convoys, ship
  A *1:* 66
  P 44–46, 48
Copenhagen
  A *1:* 46
Coral Sea, Battle of (*See* Battle
  of the Coral Sea)
Corregidor
  A *1:* 96–97, 97 (ill.), *2:* 327
  B 140
Correspondents, war
  A *2:* 285–86
Cotentin peninsula
  A *2:* 259, 268
Counter-intelligence and
  intelligence
  A *2:* 345–59
Cousins, Norman
  P 139
Crete
  A *1:* 76
Crimean Peninsula
  A *2:* 242
Croatia
  A *1:* 74, 153–56
Crystal Night (*See* Kristallnacht)
Curfew
  A *1:* 137, 141
Curzon Line
  A *2:* 216
Czechoslovakia
  A *1:* 21–23, 23 (ill.)
  B 15, 109, 225
  P 31, 102
Czechoslovakia, resistance in
  A *1:* 141, 143–45

D

Dachau concentration camp
  A *1:* 16 (ill.), *2:* 301
  B 270

Daladier, Edouard
  A *1:* 22
Danzig
  A *1:* 23, 35, 36 (ill.)
  P 32
Darlan, Admiral Jean François
  A *2:* 230–31, 231 (ill.)
  B 67
"A Date Which Will Live in
    Infamy"
  P 62–64
Davies, Joseph E.
  A *2:* 384
Davis, Benjamin O., Jr.
  B 43–52, 43 (ill.), 50 (ill.)
  A *1:* 117
Davis, Benjamin O., Sr.
  B 53–61, 53 (ill.), 60 (ill.)
Day of Infamy
  B 241
  P 62–64
D-Day
  A *2:* 251–67, 253 (ill.), 260 (ill.),
    278, 347
  B 31, 67, 77, 78, 110, 118, 152-
    153, 153 (ill.), 154, 163, 164,
    197, 200, 211, 230, 243
  P 173–86, 178 (ill.), 180 (ill.),
    184 (ill.)
de Gaulle-Anthonioz, Genevieve
  B 70
de Gaulle, Charles
  A *1:* 146, *2:* 213–15, 214 (ill.),
    230, 272
  B 62–72, 62 (ill.), 65 (ill.)
de Guingand, Francis
  B 162, 165
Death camps
  A *1:* 172–73
  P 103, 112
"The Death of Captain Waskow"
  P 147–51
Death march, Bataan
  A *1:* 97
Death march, from Auschwitz
  A *2:* 297
Death march, from Dachau
  A *2:* 301
Defense Stamps
  A *1:* 108
Denazification
  A *2:* 399

Denmark
  A *1:* 46
Denmark, and U.S. defense of
    Greenland
  A *1:* 66
Denmark, anti-German strikes in
  A *1:* 143
Denmark, non-violent resistance
    in
  A *1:* 142
Denmark, underground
    newspapers
  A *1:* 138
Deportation, of Jews
  A *1:* 172–73
  P 102–12, 106 (ill.)
Depression (economic)
  A *1:* 8–10, 9 (ill.)
Desert Fox (*See* Rommel, Erwin)
Desert War
  A *1:* 69–72
Destination Tokyo
  A *2:* 385
Destroyers for bases agreement
    (1940)
  A *1:* 64–65
Detroit, migration to
  A *1:* 108, 118
Detroit riot (June 1943)
  A *1:* 118
Dewey, Thomas
  B 286
DeWitt, John L.
  A *1:* 127
Die Grosse Liebe (*The Great Love*)
  A *2:* 378
Dieppe
  A *2:* 256–57
Discrimination, against African
    Americans
  A *1:* 114–18
  B 44-47, 49, 53, 56, 57, 59, 60,
Discrimination, against Japanese
    Americans
  A *1:* 125–29
  B 130–35
  P 85–95, 86 (ill.)
Discrimination, against Jews
  A *1:* 157–79
Discrimination, in U.S. armed
    services
  A *1:* 114–17

Distinguished Flying Cross,
    Jacqueline Cochran awarded
    B 42
Distinguished Flying Cross,
    Tuskegee Airmen awarded
    B 50
Distinguished Service Medal,
    Frank Capra awarded
    B 9
Distinguished Service Medal,
    George S. Patton awarded
    B 196
Distinguished Service Medal,
    Jacqueline Cochran awarded
    B 40
Distinguished Service Order,
    Bernard Montgomery
    awarded
    B 158
Distinguished Unit Citations,
    Tuskegee Airmen awarded
    B 50
Dodge, Chee
    B 177
Dönitz, Admiral Karl
    A *2:* 304
    P 45
Donovan, William J. "Wild Bill"
    A *2:* 354
Doolittle, General James
    A *1:* 101
    B 274
Double-Cross System
    A *2:* 349
Double-V campaign
    A *1:* 113
Dover
    A *2:* 259
Draft, military
    A *1:* 106
Draft, military, of women
    (Britain)
    A *1:* 197
Draper, Teddy, Sr. (Navajo Code
    Talker)
    B 180
Dresden, air raid
    A *1:* 191–93, 192 (ill.)
Drôle de guerre
    A *1:* 44
Dulles, Allen
    A *2:* 206 (ill.), 354, 354 (ill.)

Dumas, Sister Edwige
    B 70
Dunkirk
    A *1:* 49 (ill.), 51–53, 51 (ill.), 52
    (ill.)
    B 160
Dutch East Indies
    A *1:* 85, 99–100

E

East Africa, Italian campaign in
    A *1:* 69
East Asia
    A *1:* 28 (ill.), 84 (ill.)
East Prussia
    A *1:* 35, *2:* 296–97, 402–03
Eastern front
    A *1:* 77–82, *2:* 238–49, 243
    (ill.), 278–81, 281 (ill.)
Economic policy, in occupation
    of western Europe
    A *1:* 135
Economic policy, in occupied
    Poland
    A *1:* 133
Economy, U.S.
    A *1:* 105–08
Edelweiss Pirates
    A *1:* 204
Egypt
    A *1:* 69, 72, *2:* 227
Eiffel Tower
    A *2:* 273
834th Signal Services
    Photographic Detachment
    B 4
8th Army (British)
    A *2:* 227
    B 157, 162, 226, 228
82nd Airborne Division (U.S.)
    A *2:* 263
Einsatzgruppen
    A *1:* 134, 162, 170
Einstein, Albert
    A *2:* 366
    P 124 (ill.), 126
Eisenhower, Dwight D.
    A *2:* 262, 263 (ill.), 292, 304,
    341,
    B 59, 73 (ill.), **73–81**, 78 (ill.),
    118, 119 (ill.), 154, 164, 199,
    228, 243

P 174, 181 (ill.),182, 183, 185, 194
El Alamein
    A *2:* 227–28
    B 162, 228
Emperor of Japan (*See* Hirohito)
Emperor-system (Japan)
    A *2:* 337
Enabling Act
    A *1:* 17
England (*See* Great Britain)
English Channel
    A *1:* 50, *2:* 253 (ill.), 254
Enigma
    A *2:* 358
Enola Gay
    P 130, 131, 131 (ill.), 213
Enrico Fermi Award
    B 192
Enterprise, USS
    A *1:* 103
Ernie's War: The Best of Ernie Pyle's World War II Dispatches
    P 147–55
    (*See also* Pyle, Ernie)
Estonia
    A *1:* 38, 151, 403
Ethiopia
    A *1:* 13, 69
Europe, borders before WWII
    P 8 (map)
European Recovery Act (*See* Marshall Plan)
Evacuations, from London
    A *1:* 200–03, 203 (ill.)
Executive Order 8802 (Fair Employment Practices)
    A *1:* 113
    P 81
Executive Order 9066
    A *1:* 127
    B 130, 131
    P 86, 87
Executive Order 9981
    B 51, 61, 286
Extermination camps
    A *1:* 173

F

Fair Deal
    B 286

Fair Employment Practices Act
    P 82
Fair Employment Practices Commission (FEPC)
    A *1:* 113
Fairall, Evangeline Bakke
    P 164–66
Fascism
    A *1:* 10–13
    B 169, 170, 171
"Fat Man"
    B 190
    P 118, 121 (ill.), 126, 138
Federation of American Scientists
    P 141
Fermi, Enrico
    A *2:* 366
    B 185–87, 187 (ill.), 190
    P 118, 126
Fifth Marine Regiment
    P 198
"The Fighting Dude"
    B 138
Fighting France (*See* Free French Movement)
The Fighting Lady
    A *2:* 379
The Fighting Seabees
    A *2:* 385
Film (*See* motion pictures)
Final solution
    A *1:* 172
    B 109
    P 102, 103
Finland
    A *2:* 226, 279
Firestorm
    A *1:* 190, 192
1st Marine Division (U.S)
    A *2:* 316
    P 198
First SS Panzer Division
    P 194
First United States Army Group (FUSAG)
    A *2:* 348
    B 153, 199
"Five-Year Plan"
    B 249
Flag raising at Iwo Jima
    A *2:* 329 (ill.)
Forced labor
    A *1:* 138–39, 165–66

442nd Regimental Combat
    Team (Nisei)
    A *1:* 129
    B 132
    P 94, 94 (ill.)
Fourcade, Marie-Madeleine
    A *2:* 354–55
4th Infantry Division (U.S.)
    A *2:* 265, 274
France, Allied invasion of
    A *2:* 251–67, 253 (ill.), 260 (ill.),
        278, 347
    B 31, 67, 77, 78, 110, 118,
        152–53, 153 (ill.), 154, 163,
        164, 197, 200, 211, 230, 243
    P 173–86, 178 (ill.), 180 (ill.),
        184 (ill.)
France, defeat of (1940)
    A *1:* 53–55
France, destruction in
    A *2:* 394
France, German invasion of
    A *1:* 49 (ill.), 49–53
    B 64, 65, 160
France, losses in the war
    A *2:* 392
France, rationing in
    A *1:* 136
France, resistance in
    A *1:* 145–47
France, under occupation
    A *1:* 135–49
France, underground newspapers
    A *1:* 138
France Combatante (*See* Fighting
    French)
Franco, Francisco
    A *1:* 13, 21 *2:* 224
Frank, Hans
    A *1:* 133
Free French movement
    A *2:* 146, 213, 230
    B 66–67
French Indochina
    A *1:* 84, 88
French navy, scuttling of fleet at
    Toulon
    A *2:* 232
French resistance
    A *1:*140 (ill.), 146, 150 (ill.),
        2: 213, 230, 354–55
    B 67–68, 70
Frisch, Otto
    A *2:* 365

Fumimaro, Konoye
    B 273
FUSAG (*See* First United States
    Army Group)

G

Gable, Clark
    B 5
Gandhi, Mohandas
    A *2:* 416
Garson, Greer
    A *2:* 381
Gas chambers
    A *1:* 177, 179
    P 103, 105 (ill.)
Gasoline, rationing of
    A *1:* 110
Gaulle, Charles de (*See* de Gaulle,
    Charles)
Gdansk (*See* Danzig)
General Government (Poland)
    A *1:* 133
General Winter
    A *1:* 82
Generals' Plot (*See* Plot to kill
    Hitler)
German air force (*See* Luftwaffe)
German army, and attack on
    Poland
    A *1:* 38–43, 42 (ill.)
German army, children in
    A *2:* 304 (ill.)
German army, in Africa
    A *1:* 70–72, *2:* 227–28, 231–33
German army, in Greece
    A *1:* 73–76, 74 (ill.)
German army, in Italy
    A *2:* 233, 236–38
German army, in Russia
    A *1:* 77–81, 78 (ill.), 80 (ill.),
        2: 238–40, 241–49, 246 (ill.)
German surrender
    A *2:* 304
    B 165, 243, 255, 282
    P 214–15
Germany, after World War I
    A *1:* 4–22
Germany, air raids in
    A *1:*189–92
Germany, Allies in
    A *2:*295–304, 302 (ill.)

Germany, border changes (1945)
A *1:* 5 (ill.), 36 (ill.), *2:* 402 (ill.),
403
Germany, children in
A *1:* 203–04
Germany, civilians wounded in
air raids in
A *2:* 394
Germany, destruction in
A *2:* 395
Germany, division of
A *2:* 396, 398 (ill.)
Germany first (U.S. war strategy):
A *1:* 103–04, 307–08, 311
Germany, home front
A *1:*122–24
Germany, industrial production in
A *1:* 193
Germany, losses in the war
A *2:* 393
Germany, Morgenthau Plan
A *2:* 396
Germany, relations with other
Axis powers
A *2:* 224–26
Germany, treaty with Japan
(Anti-Comintern Pact)
(1936)
A *1:* 32
Germany, treaty with the Soviet
Union (Nazi-Soviet Pact)
A *1:* 37–38, 76
Gestapo
A *1:* 160, 204, *2:* 290, 349,
355–56
B 67, 85, 107, 108, 268
Ghetto, Warsaw uprising (1943)
A *2:* 286
Ghettos (Poland)
A *1:* 165–67, 167 (ill.)
GI Bill (Servicemen's
Readjustment Act of 1944)
A *2:* 405–06
Gilbert islands
A *1:* 95, *2:* 319
Gillars, Mildred (Axis Sally)
A *2:* 372, 373 (ill.)
Giraud, General Henri
A *2:* 214–15, 214 (ill.)
B 67
Goebbels, Joseph
A *2:* 373–74, 383
B 104–05, 105 (ill.)

Gold Beach (D-Day)
A *2:* 260, 260 (ill.), 264–65
P 174
Göring, Hermann
A *2:* 386
B 82–91, 82 (ill.), 89 (ill.)
"Gothic Line" (Italy)
A *2:* 233 (ill.), 238
Government Code and Cipher
School (Bletchley Park)
A *2:* 358
Government-in-exile, Polish
A *2:* 218–19, 282
Government-in-exile,
Netherlands
A *1:* 85
Graf Spee
A *1:* 45
Grafenort
P 112
"Grand Alliance"
A *2:* 207
Great Britain
A *1:* 21–22, 61–70, 88, *2:* 210,
253 (ill.)
Great Britain, and the Battle of
Britain
A *1:* 55–60, 185–86
Great Britain, and the Blitz
A *1:* 58–60
Great Britain, evacuations from
London
A *1:* 199–202
Great Britain, home front
A *1:* 122, 124
Great Britain, losses in the war
A *2:* 393
Great Britain, relations with other
Allied countries
A *2:* 206–13
Great Depression
A *1:* 8–9
B 3, 206, 232, 235, 241, 243
P 6, 25, 71
Great Marianas Turkey Shoot
A *2:* 320
Greater East Asia Coprosperity
Sphere
A *1:* 100
Greece, and Italian army
A *2:* 225
Greece, execution of hostages
by Germans
A *1:* 142

Greece, German invasion of
  A *1:* 73–75
Greece, Italian invasion of
  A *1:* 72–73
Greece, losses in the war
  A *2:* 392
Greece, under occupation
  A *1:* 136
Greece, withdrawal of German
    troops from
  A *2:* 299
Greenland
  A *1:* 66
Grossen-Wannsee Conference
    (*See* Wannsee Conference)
Groves, General Leslie R.
  A *2:* 367 (ill.)
  B 188
  P 118
Grynszpan, Hershel
  A *1:* 160
Guadalcanal
  A *2:* 314 (ill.), 314-316
  P 66
Guadalcanal, and Navajo
    code-talkers
  A *2:* 358
Guadalcanal Diary
  A *2:* 385
Guam
  A *1:* 95, *2:* 320
  P 61, 65
Guernica (Spain), bombing of
  A *1:* 21
Guerrilla warfare, in Ethiopia
  A *1:* 69
Guerrilla warfare, in occupied
    Europe
  A *1:*144–47, 149–52, 155–56
Gulags
  B 245, 250, 251
"Gustav Line" (Italy)
  A *2:* 233 (ill.), 236

H

Hall, Lieutenant Charles B.
  B 48
Halsey, Admiral William
  A *2:* 313
Hamburg, Germany
  A *1:* 190–91, 191 (ill.)
Hanford, Washington
  A *2:* 366

"Harlem Regiment"
  B 57
Harlem riot (August 1943)
  A *1:* 118
Harris, Air Marshall Sir Arthur
  A *1:* 189, 189 (ill.)
Hawaii (*See* Pearl Harbor)
H-Bomb
  B 191
Health and disease, in occupied
    Europe
  A *1:* 137
Hedgerows (Normandy)
  A *2:* 268, 269 (ill.)
Heisenberg, Werner
  A *2:* 364
Hepburn, Katherine
  A *2:* 378
Here Is Your War
  B 209
Heydrich, Reinhard
  A *1:* 141, 164–65,
    165 (ill.), 172
Hibakusha
  P 132, 135 (ill.), 136,
    137 (ill.), 138
Himmler, Heinrich
  A *1:* 134, 172
  B 86–87, 87 (ill.)
Hindenburg, Paul von
  A *1:* 13–14, 18
  B 106, 108
Hirohito
  A *1:* 25, *2:* 335–37, 339–40
  B **92–99**, 92 (ill.), 275
Hiroshima, Japan
  A *2:* 224, 337–38, 338 (ill.), 340
  B 97, 190, 276, 281, 285
  P 123, 125, 130–42, 137 (ill.),
    213
*The Hiroshima Maidens: A Story of
    Courage, Compassion, and
    Survival*
  P 131 (ill.) **133–38**
Hiroshima Peace Memorial
  P 141
Hitchcock, Alfred
  A *2:* 379
Hitler, Adolf
  A *1:* 10–18, 19 (ill.), 20 (ill.), 54,
    54 (ill.), 73, 76, 133, 157, *2:*
    210, 240–41 (ill.), 245, 256,
    273, 303, 349, 356

B 14, 15, 28, 82, 84, 85, 88, 100 (ill.), **100–12**, 107 (ill.), 123, 167, 171, 173, 224-26, 228, 230, 251, 259, 267, 268
P 5, 6, 21, 25, 28 (ill.), **31–41**, 32 (ill.), 101, 102, 140, 213

Hitler, Adolf, plot to kill
A *2:* 287–90
B 110, 229

Hitler Youth
A *1:* 204, *2:* 304 (ill.)
B 108, 225, 267

"Hitler's Order of the Day to the German Troops on the Eastern Front"
P **34–37**

Hitler-Stalin Pact (*See* Nazi-Soviet Pact)

HMS *Prince of Wales*
A *1:* 98

HMS *Repulse*
A *1:* 98

Hobby, Oveta Culp
B **113–20**, 113 (ill.), 119 (ill.)

Hoftiezer, Myrtle Brethouwer
P 166–67

Hollywood
A *2:* 378–79, 383
B 4

Holocaust
A *1:* 157–79, 158 (ill.), 163 (ill.) 167 (ill.), 169 (ill.), 175 (ill.), 178 (ill.), 202
B 109, 256
P 35, 101–16, 105 (ill.), 106 (ill.), 113 (ill.)

The Holocaust Lady
P 109

Home front
A *1:* 105–29
P 69–85

Home Army (Polish)
A *1:* 35, *2:* 282–86

Hong Kong
A *1:* 95

Honshu
A *2:* 332

Hood, HMS
P 46, 46 (ill.), 48

Hoover, Herbert
P 24, 25

Hornet USS (*See* USS *Hornet*)

Hull, Cordell
P 62, 64

Hungarian army
A *1:* 78

Hungary
A *1:* 74, 135 *2:* 220, 225, 244, 298, 393

Hunger winter (Netherlands)
A *1:* 136

I

I Am an American: A True Story of Japanese Internment
P **89–92**

I Saw Hitler!
B 267

"I Thought It Was the End"
P **151–52**

Iceland
A *1:* 66

Ie Shima
A *2:* 388
B 213–14
P 146, 149

Ikoku, Iva Toguri (TokyoRose)
A *2:* 373

Il Duce (*See* Mussolini, Benito)

The Immortal Sergeant
A *2:* 385

Imperialism
A *1:* 27

In Solitary Witness: The Life and Death of Franz Jaggerstatter
B 126

Incendiary bombs
A *1:* 188

India
A *1:* 61, 62 (ill.), 99, *2:* 208, 393, 412, 415 (ill.), 416

India, and the Bengal famine (1943)
A *2:* 412

Indochina
A *1:* 84, *2:* 416

Indonesia
A *1:* 85, *2:* 415
(*See also* Dutch East Indies)

Industry, American
A *1:*66, 106–08, 109 (ill.), 111–12

Industry, women in
A *1:* 119–24, 119 (ill.), 120 (ill.)

Infantry Attacks
B 224

Inouye, Daniel Ken
 B 132–33, 133 (ill.)
 P 94
Intelligence
 A 2: 345–59
International Military Tribunal
 (*See* Nuremberg trials)
Internment, (*See* Japanese
 American internment)
*Iron Coffins: A Personal Account of
 the German U-Boat Battles of
 World War II*
 P 48–55
Iron Cross, Erwin Rommel
 awarded
 B 224
Iron Cross, Hanna Reitsch
 awarded
 B 39
Iron Curtain
 B 32
Ironbottom Sound (Guadalcanal)
 A 2: 315
Island hopping strategy
 A 2: 307–10, 318
Isolationism
 A 1: 6, 62–63
 B 218, 254
 P 21
It's A Wonderful Life
 A 2: 379
 B 8 (ill.), 9
Italian Americans
 A 1: 127
Italian army
 A 1:69, 72–73, 78, 2: 234
Italian Socialist Republic
 A 2: 235
 B 174
Italy
 A 1: 12, 69, 72–73, 74, 144,
 154,2: 220, 244
Italy, Allied invasion of
 A 2: 233 (ill.), 233–38, 234 (ill.),
 251
 B 30, 163, 173, 174, 228, 242,
 266
 P 144, 147–52, 150 (ill.), 156
Italy, declaration of war against
 Germany (1943)
 A 2: 236
Italy, losses in the war
 A 2: 393

Italy, relations with Germany
 A 2: 224–25, 235
Italy, rise of Fascism
 A 1: 12
Iwo Jima
 A 1: 195, 2: 309 (ill.), 326 (ill.),
 327 (ill.), 327–28, 329 (ill.)
 B 180
 P 119–20, 144–45, 145 (ill.),
 204

J

Jaggerstatter, Franz
 B 121–28
Japan
 A 1: 25–26, 27, 32 (ill.), 84,
 195, 2: 222, 333 (ill.)
 P 119, 129–32, 130 (map),
 144–46, 54 (map)
Japan, and Germany
 A 2: 224
Japan, and Soviet Union
 A 1: 37, 87, 2: 220
Japan, before World War II
 A 1: 24–27
Japan, losses in the war
 A 2: 410
Japan, negotiations with U.S.
 (1941)
 A 1: 88
Japan, occupation of French
 Indochina
 A 1: 85
Japan, seizes Manchuria (1931)
 A 1: 29
Japan, surrender of
 A 2: 339–40, 343 (ill.), 344
 B 97, 143, 190, 276, 285
 P 215–20, 215 (ill.), 216 (ill.)
Japan, treaty with Nazi Germany
 (Anti-Comintern Pact) (1936)
 A 1: 32
Japan, war crimes trials
 A 2: 410
Japan, war with China (1937–45)
 A 1: 32–34
Japanese American Internment
 A 1: 127–29
 B 129–35, 243
 P 85–95, 93 (ill.)
Japanese American soldiers
 A 1:129

B 132–33
P 94, 94 (ill.)
Japanese Americans
A *1:* 125–29
B 129–35
P 85–95, 86 (ill.), 88 (ill.), 90 (ill.)
Japanese army, and atrocities in China
A *1:* 30, 32
Japanese-Soviet Neutrality Treaty (1941)
A *1:* 87
Jasenovac concentration camp
A *1:* 154
Java
A *1:* 99
Java Sea, Battle of
A *1:* 99
Jeannette Rankin Brigade
B 221
Jewish Council (*Judenrat*)
A *1:* 165–66
Jewish star
A *1:* 166, 172
Jews, and building of atomic bomb
A *2:* 366
Jews, and German occupation policies
A *1:* 132, 162–63, 163 (ill.)
Jews, and German propaganda
A *2:* 371
Jews, and Hollywood
A *2:* 381
Jews, and the Holocaust
A *1:* 157–79, 158 (ill.), 175 (ill.), 178 (ill.)
B 109, 256
P 35, 101–16, 105 (ill.), 106 (ill.), 113 (ill.)
Jews, Eastern European
A *1:* 77
Jews, Finnish
A *2:* 279
Jews, Nazi racial theories concerning
A *1:* 77
Jews, Polish
A *2:* 392
Jews, Russian
A *1:* 168–70, 169 (ill.)
Johnston, Philip
B 176–78

Joyce, William (Lord Haw Haw)
A *2:* 372
Jud Süss
A *2:* 375
Judenrat (*See* Jewish Council)
July Plot
A *2:* 287–90
Juno Beach (D-Day)
A *2:* 260, 260 (ill.), 264–65
P 174

K

Kaiser (German Emperor), abdication of
A *1:* 4
Kamenev, Lev
B 249
Kamikaze
A *2:* 325, 329, 331–32
P 119, 140, 146, 206
Kasserine Pass
A *2:* 232
Katyn Massacre
A *2:* 218–19
Kenya
A *1:* 69
Khan, Noor Inayat
A *2:* 355
Kharkov
A *2:* 242, 247
Kiev
A *1:* 78, 171, *2:* 248
Kindertransporte
A *1:* 202
King, Admiral Ernest
A *2:* 310
Kirkpatrick, Helen
A *2:* 387
Klisura, Greece
A *1:* 142
Knight's Cross, Erwin Rommel awarded
B 226
Know Your Enemy—Japan
B 8
Kolberg
A *2:* 376
Kolombangara
A *2:* 318
Kolomyja
A *1:* 174

Korea
  A *1:* 27–28, 31
Korean War (1950–53)
  B 24, 79, 144, 145, 155, 287
  P 123, 219
Korematsu, Fred T.
  B **129–35**, 129 (ill.), 134 (ill.)
Kovno, Lithuania
  A *1:* 170–71
Kremlin
  A *1:* 81
Kretschmer, Otto
  P 55
Kriegsmarine
  P 44, 45
Kristallnacht
  A *1:* 160
  B 105, 260
Kulmhof concentration camp
    (*See* Chelmno concentration
    camp)
Kuomintang (Chinese Nationalist
    Party)
  A *1:* 33, *2:* 411
  B 17-19, 21, 22, 154
Kursk
  A *2:* 247–49
  B 252, 254
Kursk salient
  A *2:* 247–48
Kwajalein
  A *2:* 320
Kyushu, planned invasion of
  A *2:* 332

L

Labor camps
  A *1:* 166
The Lady Vanishes
  A *2:* 379
Lake, Veronica
  A *1:* 121
Lang, Fritz
  A *2:* 383
Latin America, U.S. influence in
  A *2:* 208
Latvia
  A *1:* 38, 76, 151, *2:* 403
Laval, Pierre
  A *1:* 148
Lawrence, Ernest
  B 190

Le Duc, Marie-Louise
  B 70
League of German Girls
  A *1:* 204
League of Nations
  A *1:* 6, *2:* 408
  B 108, 171
Leahy, William D.
  A *2:* 341
Leander, Zarah
  A *2:* 378
Leapfrogging strategy
  B 142, 176
Lebensraum
  A *1:* 76, 132
Leclerc, Phillip
  A *2:* 274
Leipzig
  A *1:* 161
Lend-Lease Act (March 1941)
  A *1:* 65, 87, 106, *2:* 207, 213
  B 21, 30, 38, 151, 240
  P 23, 24
Lenin, Vladimir Ilich
  A *1:* 81
  B 246–49
  P 38
Leningrad
  A *1:* 81, *2:* 377, 392
Leningrad Symphony
    (Shostakovitch)
  A *2:* 377
Levittown, NY
  A *2:* 407 (ill.)
Lewis, John L.
  A *1:* 112
Lexington, *USS (*See *USS*
    Lexington)
Leyte Gulf
  A *2:* 324–26
The Liberation of Rome
  A *2:* 379
Liberty ships
  A *1:* 66, 67 (ill.)
Libya
  A *1:* 69, 70, *2:* 227
Liddell Hart, B. H.
  A *1:* 188, *2:* 216
Lidice, Czechoslovakia
  A *1:* 141
Life in a Jewish Family
  B 257
Lindbergh, Charles
  A *1:* 63

Lithuania
    A *1:* 38, 76, 151, 170, *2:* 280, 403
"Little Boy"
    B 190
    P 118, 121 (ill.), 126, 131, 138
Litvak, Anatole
    A *2:* 379
    B 6
Litvak, Lily
    A *1:* 197
Lockbourne Air Base
    B 51
Lodz ghetto
    A *1:* 166–68
London, bombing of
    A *1:* 57–60, 182 (ill.), 186
    B 206
London, evacuation
    A199–202, 203 (ill.)
    P 16 (ill.)
London Poles
    A *2:* 218, 282–86
London to Ladysmith via Pretoria
    B 27
London, V-1 bombing of
    A *2:* **361**
Lord Haw Haw (*See* Joyce, William)
Los Alamos, New Mexico
    A *2:* 367
    B 183, 189, 282
    P 118
Los Angeles, migration to
    A *1:* 108
Los Angeles, riots (June 1943)
    A *1:* 118
Louis, Joe
    A *1:* 117
Lovelace, Randolph
    B 36
Lübeck, Germany
    A *1:* 188
Lublin Committee
    A *2:* 219, 283
Lublin, Poland
    A *1:* 173–74, *2:* 280
Luftwaffe
    A *1:* 42, 47–48, 52–53, 56,
        74, 76–77, 182–83, 185–86
        2: 240, 245, 253
    B 39, 88
    P 144, 173
Luxembourg
    A *2:* 292, 396

Luzon, Philippines
    A *1:* 96, *2:* 326
Lvov, Poland
    A *1:* 173, *2:* 280

M

MacArthur, General Douglas
    A *1:* 95–98, *2:* 312, 313, 324,
        344, 410
    B 76, 77, 97, 98, 136 (ill.),
        136–46, 143 (ill.), 276, 287
    P 214, 215 (ill.) 218–20
Madame Chiang Kai-Shek
    B 19, 20
Magic (American interception of
    Japanese codes)
    A *2:* 357
Maginot Line
    A *1:* 48–50, 49 (ill.)
Malaya
    A *1:* 97
Malaysia
    A *1:* 97
Malmédy massacre
    A *2:* 293, 294 (ill.), 295 (ill.)
    P 194
Manchukuo
    A *1:* 30–31
Manchuria
    A *1:* 28–29, *2:* 221–22, 333,
        342, 339, 411
Manhattan District of the Army
    Corps of Engineers
    A *2:* 366
Manhattan Project
    A *2:* 223, 365–68
    B 186–89, 191, 241
    P 117–28
Manila
    A *1:* 96, *2:* 326
Manzanar
    A *1:* 129
    P 89–93, 93 (ill.)
Mao Tse-tung
    B 154
Mao Zedong
    A *2:* 413 (ill.)
Maquis fighting groups
    A *1:* 140 (ill.)
    B 68
March on Washington Movement
    A *1:* 112

Marco Polo Bridge
  B 21
Mariana Islands
  A *2:* 320, 323, 326 (ill.)
Marine Corps (U.S.), and African
    Americans
  A *1:* 114–15, 117
Marine Corps (U.S.), at
    Guadalcanal
  A *2:* 313–16, 314 (ill.)
Marine Corps (U.S.), at Iwo Jima
  A *2:* 309 (ill.), 327–28
Marine Corps (U.S.), at Okinawa
  A *2:* 328–32, 330 (ill.), 331 (ill.)
Marine Corps (U.S.), at Tarawa
  A *2:* 319
Marine Corps Monument to Iwo
    Jima
  A *2:* 328
Marseille
  A *2:* 271
Marshall, General George C.
  A *1:* 114, *2:* 209–11
  B 3, 22, 75, 114, **147–56,**
    147 (ill.)
Marshall Islands
  A *2:* 319–20
Marshall Plan
  B 154–55, 285
Marx, Karl
  P 38
Marxism
  P 38, 39
Massacre at Malmédy (*See*
    Malmédy massacre)
Master race
  A *1:* 157
Mauldin, Bill
  A *2:* 389, 389 (ill.)
  B 207
McAuliffe, Anthony
  P 193
McNair, Lieutenant Lesley James
  B 46
Medical experiments
  A *1:* 179
Meiji Restoration
  A *1:* 26
Mein Kampf
  B 102, 103
*Memoirs by Harry S. Truman
    Volume 1: Year of Decisions*
  B 288
  P 120–25, 214–20

Memorial Day Massacre
  A *1:* 105
Meredith, Burgess
  A *2:* 390
Meuse River
  A *1:* 49
Mexican Americans
  A *1:* 118
Midway, Battle of (*See* Battle of
    Midway)
Midway Island (*See* Battle of
    Midway)
Migration
  A *1:* 108
Mihailovic, Draza
  A *1:* 153, 154, 156
Mike, King (Navajo Code Talker)
  B 179
Milice (France)
  A *1:* 148
Militarism, Japanese
  A *1:* 30–31, 83 *2:* 410
Miller, Dorie
  A *1:* 118
  B 58, 59 (ill.)
Mines
  A *2:* 255, 265, 334
Minsk, liberation of
  A *2:* 280
Mission to Moscow
  A *2:* 384
Missouri, *USS* (See *USS* Missouri*)
Momyer, Colonel William
  B 49
Monte Cassino (*See* Cassino)
Montenegro
  A *1:* 154–55
Montevideo
  A *1:* 45
Montgomery, General Bernard L.
  A *2:* 228, 233, 235, 252, 291,
    299
  B 157–66, 157 (ill.), 164 (ill.),
    201, 227
  P 146, 174, 193
The Moon is Down
  A *2:* 383
Moravia
  A *1:* 23
Morocco
  A *2:* 228–30
Mortain counter-offensive
  A *2:* 359

Moscow, Battle of
  A *1:* 81
Motion pictures, American
  A *2:* 378–85
  (*See also* Hollywood)
Motion pictures, German
  A *2:* 374
Motion pictures, in occupied
    Europe
  A *1:* 137
Mount Suribachi, Iwo Jima
  A *2:* 328
  P 145, 145 (ill.)
Mountbatten, Admiral Louis
  A *2:* 415 (ill.)
  B 160
Mr. Citizen
  B 288
Mrs. Miniver
  A *2:* 380, 382
Mulberries (artificial harbors)
  A *2:* 258–259, 259 (illus.)
Münchhausen
  A *2:* 378
Munich Beer Hall Putsch
  B 84, 85, 103
Munich Conference
  A *1:* 21
Munich Pact
  B 14
Murmansk
  A *2:* 213
Murphy, Audie
  B 5
Muslims (Bosnian), persecution
    by Ustashi of
  A *1:* 154
Mussolini, Benito
  A *1:* 12, 21, 53, 69, 72, *2:* 224,
    234–35
  B **167–74**, 14, 109, 167 (ill.),
    172 (ill.), 228
  P 21, 28 (ill.), 213
Mustang (American fighter plane)
  A *1:* 194
My Struggle (*See* Mein Kampf)
Myanmar
  A *1:* 99

N

Nacht und Nebel (Night and Fog)
  A *1:* 142

Nagasaki, Japan
  A *2:* 224, 338, 340 (ill.)
  B 97, 190, 276, 281, 285
  P 123, 125, 126, 130, 136, 138,
    139 (ill.), 140, 213
Nanking, Rape of
  A *1:* 32
  B 273
Nantes
  A *1:* 142
Naples, liberation of
  A *2:* 236
Narvik
  A *1:* 46, 46 (ill.)
National Socialist German
    Workers' Party (*See*
    Nazi Party)
Nationalism
  P 5, 35
Nationalist Party, China
    (*See* Kuomintang)
Nationalist Party, Germany
  A *1:* 17–18
Native Americans
  A *2:* 358, 359 (ill.)
  B **175–82**, 175 (ill.), 181 (ill.)
Navajo Code Talkers
  A *2:* 358, 359 (ill.)
  B **175–82**, 175 (ill.), 181 (ill.)
Navy, British, and blockade of
    Germany in World War I
  A *1:* 4
Navy, British, in Battle of the
    Atlantic
  A *1:* 66
Navy, Canadian, in Battle of
    the Atlantic
  A *1:* 66
Nazi Party
  A *1:* 10–18
  B 84, 85, 100, 103, 105, 106,
    107, 108, 121, 122, 224, 259,
    260, 263, 267, 268
  P 5–6, 27, 35, 37, 101–02
The Nazis Strike
  B 7
Nazi-Soviet Nonaggression Pact
    (1939)
  A *1:* 37–38 (ill.), 43, 76,
    2: 215, 283
  P 6, 17, 22, 32
The Negro Soldier
  B 8, 58

Nehru, Jawaharlal
  A *2:* 415 (ill.), 416
Netherlands
  A *2:* 396
Netherlands, and Dutch East
    Indies (Indonesia)
  A *1:* 85
Netherlands, invasion of
  A *1:* 47
Netherlands, resistance in
  A *1:* 138, 139, 142, 143
Netherlands, under occupation
  A *1:* 136, 141, *2:* 392, 394
Networks, intelligence
  A *2:* 352–353
Nevada, USS (*See* USS *Nevada*)
New Britain
  A *2:* 317, 319
New Deal
  B 232, 235–39, 243, 280, 286
  P 25
New Georgia
  A *2:* 317
New Guinea
  A *1:* 101, *2:* 317 (ill.), 318,
    321, 323
New Ireland
  A *2:* 319
New Order
  A *2:* 371
The New Russia
  B 265
Newfoundland, meeting of
    Roosevelt and Churchill
    (August 1941)
  A *2:* 207
  P 22
Newspapers, underground
  A *1:* 138
Newsreels
  A *2:* 376
Nice, Paris
  A *2:* 271
Nigeria
  A *1:* 69
Night and Fog (*See Nacht und
    Nebel*)
Night bombing by RAF
  A *1:* 187
Night of Broken Glass (*See
    Kristallnacht*)
Night witches
  A *1:* 197
Niimoto, Shigeko
  P 133, 136–38, 139

Nimitz, Admiral Chester
  A *2:* 311, 313, 316
  B 77, 141, 142
99th Fighter Squadron
  A *1:* 117
99th Pursuit Squadron
  B 47–49
92nd Infantry Division
  A *1:* 115
93rd Infantry Divisions
  A *1:* 115
Nisei
  A *1:* 125
*No Time for Fear: Voices of
    American Military Nurses in
    World War II*
  P 161–67
Noah's Ark (intelligence network)
  A *2:* 354
Nobel Peace Prize, George C.
    Marshall awarded
  B 155
Nomuri, Shiro
  P 89–92
Normandy, and the Allied
    bombing campaign
  A *1:* 189
  (*See also* D-Day)
Normandy, and Ultra
  A *2:* 359
Normandy, Battle of (June–Aug
    1944)
  A *2:* 268–71, 270 (ill.), 271 (ill.)
  (*See also* D-Day)
Normandy, France
  A *1:* 43, *2:* 253 (ill.), 260 (ill.)
    262, 269 (ill.)
  P 156, 173–86, 176 (map), 180
    (ill.), 184 (ill.), 188
  (*See also* D-Day)
Normandy, intelligence
  A *2:* 347
Normandy Invasion (*See* D-Day)
North Africa
  A *1:* 69–72, 71 (ill.), *2:* 227–33,
    229 (ill.)
  B 162, 163, 223, 226–28, 266
  P 143
North Africa, Allied invasion of
  A *2:* 211, 212 (ill.), 228–30
  B 30, 48, 67, 77, 198, 208
North Africa, Italian invasion of
  A *1:* 69–70

North Atlantic Treaty
    Organization (NATO)
    B 79, 155, 165, 285
Northern Expedition
    B 19
Norway, German invasion of
    A *1:* 45–47, 46 (ill)
Norway, German reprisals in
    A *1:* 141
No-strike pledge
    A *1:* 108, 112
"Notes from a Battered Country"
    P 147
Notre Dame Cathedral (Paris)
    A *2:* 387
Nuclear energy
    P 117, 126
Nuclear fission
    B 185
Nuremberg laws
    A *1:* 159
Nuremberg rallies
    A *2:* 374
Nuremberg trials
    A *2:* 399–401, 400 (ill.)
    B 90, 276
Nurses, U.S. Army
    A *1:* 198, 198 (ill.)
    P 159–69, 160 (ill.), 163 (ill.),
    167 (ill.), 168 (ill.)

O

Oahu
    A *1:* 89
Oak Ridge, Tennessee
    A *2:* 366
Occupation
    A *1:* 131–56
Occupation of Japan
    B 143, 144
Office of Price Administration
    and Civilian Supply (OPA)
    A *1:* 110
    P 72
Office of Production
    Management (OPM)
    A *1:* 106
Office of Strategic Services (OSS)
    A *1:* 155, *2:* 354
Office of War Information (OWI)
    A *2:* 382
Oil fields
    A *1:* 69, 73

Okinawa
    A *2:* 306, 326 (ill.), 328,
    330 (ill.), 332
    B 180–81, 213
    P 119, 120, 145, 146,
    153 (ill.), 156 (map),
    204–07, 208 (ill.), 212
"Old Blood and Guts" (*See*
    George S. Patton)
Olympic Games (Berlin 1936)
    A *2:* 374
Omaha Beach (D-Day)
    A *2:* 260, 260 (ill.), 266–67,
    267 (ill.)
    P 174, 176, 184, 184 (ill.), 185
"On the Record"
    B 268
"On Victory in Europe"
    P 155
Onderduikers (divers)
    A *1:* 140
101st Airborne Division (U.S.)
    A *2:* 263
    P 188, 193
116th Infantry Regiment of the
    29th Division
    P 174, 176
OPA (*See* Office of Price
    Administration and
    Civilian Supply)
Operation Anvil
    A *2:* 271–72, 272 (ill.)
Operation Barbarossa
    A *1:* 77
    P 33, 36 (ill.)
Operation Fortitude
    A *2:* 347–49
Operation Market Garden
    B 164
Operation Overlord (*See* D-Day)
Operation Torch
    A *2:* 211, 212 (ill.), 228
    B 30, 77, 198, 208
Oppenheimer, J. Robert
    A *2:* 367 (ill.), 367–68
    B 183–92, 183 (ill.), 188 (ill.)
    P 118
Oran
    A *2:* 228, 230
"Order of the Day to the German
    Troops on the Eastern Front"
    P 34–37
Orphans
    A *1:* 202–03

Oslo
  A *1:* 47, 46 (ill.)
Oslo Report (British intelligence)
  A *2:* 350
OSS (*See* Office of Strategic
  Services)
Overlord, Operation (*See* D-Day)
OWI (*See* Office of War
  Information)
Oxford, England
  A *2:* 358

P

Pacific ocean, islands
  A *1:* 94 (ill.), *2:* 307 (ill.)
Pacific theater
  A *2:* 306, 309, 310, 312 (ill.)
  B 140, 141, 142, 161, 175, 176,
    179, 180, 213, 214, 242, 275
  P 212 (map)
Pacifism
  B 215, 218, 220
Pact of Steel
  B 109, 173
Palau
  P 197
Panzer (tank) divisions (German)
  A *1:* 39, 77
Papua, New Guinea
  A *2:* 318, 319
Parachute troops, at D-Day
  A *2:* 260, 263 (ill.)
Parachute troops, and capture of
  Crete
  A *1:* 76
Paris, France
  A *1:* 53, 136, *2:* 271–74, 289
  B 67
  P 187
Partisans, and Operation
  Bagration (White Russia)
  A *2:* 279
Partisans, in Slovakia
  A *1:* 145
Partisans, in the Soviet Union
  A *1:* 149–52, 196–97, 196 (ill.)
Partisans, in Yugoslavia
  A *1:* 155
Partisans, liberation of Belgrade by
  A *2:* 299
Partisans, women
  A *1:* 197

Pas de Calais
  A *2:* 259, 271
Patton, George S.
  A *1:* 115, *2:* 270–71, 233, 269,
    291, 298, 301, 348, 390
  B 163, **193–202**, 193 (ill.),
    200 (ill.)
  P 146, 174, 188
Paul, Prince (Yugoslav Regent)
  A *1:* 73
Pearl Harbor Attack
  A *1:* 89–92, 91 (ill.), 92 (ill.),
    2: 345
  B 58, 59, 130, 140, 208, 241,
    243, 275
  P 26, 37, 59–68, 63 (ill.) 78, 85,
    94, 118, 140, 212
Peenemünde
  A *2:* 363
Peierls, Rudolf
  A *2:* 365
Peiper, Jochen
  P 194
Peking
  A *1:* 32
Peleliu
  P 197–204, 200 (ill.),
    205 (ill.), 207
Percival, General Sir Arthur
  A *2:* 344
Perkins, Frances
  P 28
Perry, Commodore Matthew
  A *1:* 25
Pershing, General John J.
  B 149
Petacci, Clara
  B 174
Pétain, Marshal Henri Phillippe
  A *1:* 54, 145–46
  B 64
P-51 Mustang (American fighter
  plane)
  A *1:* 194
Philippine Sea, Battle of the
  A *2:* 320
Philippines
  A *1:* 86, 95, *2:* 323–24, 324 (ill.)
  B 140, 142
  P 61, 65, 218, 219
Phony War
  A *1:* 43
Pianists (radio operators)
  A *2:* 356

Picasso, Pablo
A *1:* 21
Pike, Catherine "Renee" Young
P 71–84
Plot to kill Hitler
A *2:* 287, 289
B 110, 229
Pocketful of Miracles
B 9
Poison gas
A *1:* 194–95
Poland
A *1:* 5, 36, *2:* 215, 217, 394, 402
Poland, border changes
A *2:* 217, 217 (ill.), 403
Poland, German demands on
A *1:* 23, 35
Poland, German invasion of
A *1:* 23–24, 38–43, 42 (ill.)
B 15, 109, 151, 198, 225, 240, 269
P 7, 7 (ill.), 31–32
Poland, German occupation policies
A *1:* 133
Poland, Jewish population of
A *1:* 162
Poland, losses in the war
A *2:* 392
Poland, orphans in
A *1:* 202–03
Polish army
A *1:* 39–43
Polish Committee of National Liberation (*See* Lublin Committee)
Polish Corridor
A *1:* 6, 35, 36 (ill.)
Polish-Soviet relations
A *2:* 218, 282
Port Arthur
A *1:* 29
Port Moresby
A *2:* 318
Potsdam Conference
A *2:* 336 (ill.)
P 119, 123, 140, 221
Potsdam Declaration
A *2:* 335–37
P 125, 130, 221
Pour le Merite, Erwin Rommel awarded
B 224

Pour le Merite, Hermann Göring awarded
B 83
Poznan
A *1:* 134
Prague, Czechoslovakia
A *1:* 143
Prelude to War
A *2:* 379
B 6, 7
Presidential Medal of Freedom, Fred Korematsu awarded
B 135
Presidential Unit Citation, 761st Tank Battalion awarded
B 46
Prien, Günther
P 44, 55
Prince of Wales, HMS
A *1:* 98
Prisoners of war (POWs)
A *1:* 97, 124, 132, 139, 202
P 161, 168, 191 (ill.), 216 (ill.)
Production, industrial
A *1:* 106–08
Propaganda
A *2:* 370–71, 373
B 3, 6, 8, 68, 102, 104, 107, 169, 171
Protests, against German occupation
A *1:* 142–43
Provisional French National Committee (*See* Free French movement)
Proximity fuse
A *2:* 360
Psychological warfare
A *2:* 372
Pulitzer Prize, Bill Mauldin
A *2:* 388
Pulitzer Prize, Ernie Pyle
A *2:* 387
Purple Code
A *2:* 356, 357
The Purple Heart
A *2:* 385
Putten, Netherlands
A *1:* 141
Pyle, Ernie
A *2:* 387–88, 388 (ill.), 390
B 203–14, 203 (ill.), 212 (ill.)
P 143–57, 148 (ill.)

Q

Quebec Conference
B 243

R

Rabaul
A *2:* 317, 319
Racial theories, Nazi
A *1:* 77, 132
Racism
A *1:* 31, 96, 114–17, 125–29,
126 (ill.), 128 (ill.) *2:* 383
B 44–47, 49, 53, 56, 57, 59, 60,
87, 103, 104, 130–35
P 82, 85, 87, 91, 94, 169
Radar, and the Battle of Britain
A *1:* 56, 68, 136, *2:* 349, 360
Radiation sickness
P 136
Radio
A *2:* 372–74
Radio transmitters, and
intelligence work
A *2:* 352, 355
RAF (*See* Royal Air Force)
Raffa, Margaret Richey
P 162–64
Railroads
A *1:* 112, *2:* 394
Rains, Claude
A *2:* 382 (ill.)
Randolph, A. Philip
A *1:* 112, 113
Rangers, U.S., D-Day
A *2:* 266
Rankin, Jeannette
B **215–22**, 215 (ill.), 220 (ill.)
Rape of Nanking
A *1:* 32
B 273
Rationing
A *1:* 109–11, 110 (ill.), 136, 200
P 72–74, 73 (ill.)
Ray, Satyajit
A *2:* 412
Recruitment films
A *2:* 378
Red Army
A *1:*77–82, *2:* 240–49, 356
Red Army, and actions against
civilians (East Prussia)
A *2:* 296, 393

Red Army, and Warsaw uprising
(1944)
A *2:* 285
Red Army, and winter 1945
offensive
A *2:* 296
Red Army, Operation Bagration
A *2:* 278–82
Red Army, takes Warsaw
A *2:* 295–96
Red Ball Express
A *2:* 291
Red Orchestra (intelligence
network)
A *2:* 355–56
Red Tails" (*See* Tuskegee Airmen)
Refugees
A *1:* 159
Refugees, and atomic bomb
A *2:* 366
Refugees, and intelligence work
A *2:* 353
Refugees, in Battle of France
A *1:* 53
Refugees, in Dresden
A *1:* 192
Refugees, in East Prussia
A *2:* 296
Reich Citizenship Law
(*See* Nuremberg laws)
Reichskristallnacht
(*See* Crystal Night)
Reichstag
B 85, 106, 107
Reichstag fire
A *1:* 15, 15 (ill.)
Reims
A *2:* 304
Reitsch, Hanna
B 39
Relocation, of
Japanese-Americans
A *1:* 127–28, 128 (ill.)
B 129–35, 243
P 85–95, 86 (ill.), 88 (ill.),
90 (ill.)
Remagen, Germany
A *2:* 298
Reparations (repayments)
A *1:* 7
Replacement Army (*Ersatzheer*)
A *2:* 288
Republic of China (*See* China)

Repulse, HMS
  A *1:* 98
Reserve Police (German)
  A *1:* 174
Resistance movements
  A *1:* 139–48, 150–52, *2:* 213,
    214, 268, 352, 353, 382, 383
Resistance movements, and
    forced labor
  A *1:* 139
Resistance movements, and
    intelligence work
  A *2:* 352
Resistance movements, and
    Normandy invasion
  A *2:* 353
Resistance movements, and
    North Africa
  A *2:* 230
Resistance movements, armed
  A *1:* 144
Resistance movements, in France
  A *1:* 140 (ill.), 145–48, 150 (ill.),
    2: 213, 214, 268, 353
Resistance movements, in
    motion pictures
  A *2:* 382, 383
Resistance movements, in
    occupied Europe
  A *1:* 140 (ill.) 142–56, 150 (ill.)
Resistance movements, in Poland
  A *1:* 135
Resistance movements, in the
    Soviet Union
  A *1:* 150–52, 151 (ill.)
Reynaud, Paul
  B 64
Rhine River
  A *2:* 291, 298, 300 (ill.), 301 (ill.)
  P 194
Rhineland
  A *1:* 5, 19, 204, *2:* 241
Ribbentrop-Molotov Pact (*See*
    Nazi-Soviet Pact)
Riefenstahl, Leni
  A *2:* 374, 375 (ill.)
  B 6
Riots, Detroit (June 1943)
  A *1:* 118
Riots, Harlem (August 1943)
  A *1:* 118
Riots, Los Angeles (zoot suit riots)
  A *1:* 118
Riots, race, in military
  A *1:* 117

The River War
  B 26
Rivers, Ruben
  B 46
Roma (Gypsies)
  A *1:* 154
Romania
  A *2:* 225, 244, 298
Romania, German economic
    policy in
  A *1:* 135
Romania, losses in the war
  A *2:* 393
Rome, liberation of
  A *2:* 238
Rommel, Erwin
  A *1:* 70–71, 70 (ill.), *2:* 228,
    231, 232, 261, 290, 357
  B 223–31, 157, 162, 223 (ill.),
    227 (ill.), 242
  P 173, 176
"Rommel's asparagus"
  B 228
Roosevelt, (Anna) Eleanor
  A *2:* 378
  B 210, 233, 234, 236, 237
  P 24, 78
Roosevelt, Franklin D.
  A *1:* 63, 90, 93 (ill.), 103–04,
    113, 127, *2:* 207–10, 214–16,
    214 (ill.), 221 (ill.), 303, 341,
    365–66, 408, 414
  B 7, 22, 30, 47, 57, 140, 154,
    186, 232 (ill.), **232–44**
    242 (ill.),280–82
  P 21–30, 23 (ill.), 26 (ill.), 46,
    59–68, 65 (ill.), 71, 78, 82,
    86, 122, 126
Rose of Stalingrad
  A *1:* 197
Rosenthal, Joe (photographer)
  A *2:* 328
Rosie the Riveter
  A *1:* 119–21, 109 (ill.)
Rostock, Germany
  A *1:* 188
Rotterdam, Netherlands
  A *1:* 48, 182
Royal Air Force (RAF)
  A *1:*52, 55–59, 57 (ill.), 183–93,
    183, 184 (ill.), 187 (ill.),
    264, 380
  P 17, 173

Royal Air Force (RAF), and D-Day
   A *2:* 264
Royal Air Force (RAF), and night
      bombing of Germany
   A *1:* 187
Royal Air Force (RAF), and
      strategic bombing
   A *1:* 183
Royal Air Force (RAF), at Dunkirk
   A *1:* 52
Royal Air Force (RAF), in Battle of
      Britain
   A *1:* 55–56
Royal Canadian Air Force
   P 56 (ill.)
Rubber, synthetic
   A *1:* 107
Ruhr, Germany
   A *1:* 189, *2:* 299
Rumania
   A *2:* 225
Rumanian army
   A *1:* 78
Rundstedt Offensive (*See* Battle of
      the Bulge)
Russia (*See* Soviet Union)
Russian Revolution of 1917
   P 38
Russo-Finnish War
   A *2:* 279
Russo-Japanese War (1905)
   A *1:* 29
Ryukyu Islands
   A *2:* 326 (ill.), 328
   P 205

S

SA (*See* Storm Troopers)
Sabotage, by French resistance
   A *1:* 147 (ill.), *2:* 268
Sabotage, by young Germans
   A *1:* 203–04
Sabotage, in occupied Europe
   A *1:* 142–43
Sahara
   A *2:* 385
Saipan
   A *2:* 320, 326 (ill.), 328
Salerno
   A *2:* 236
Salo, Republic of
   B 174

Samurai
   A *1:* 30
San Diego, migration to
   A *1:* 108
Sardinia
   A *2:* 347
Saving Private Ryan
   P 185
Schultz, Sigrid
   A *2:* 385
Schutzstaffel (*See* SS)
Science
   A *2:* 359–68
Scientists, and the
      atomic bomb
   A *2:* 364–65
Scientists, German
   A *2:* 399
Scientists, Jewish
   A *2:* 366
Scientists, refugees
   A *2:* 366
Scorched earth policy
   A *1:* 80
   B 254
SD (*Sicherheitsdienst*)
   A *1:* 168
2nd Cavalry Division
   A *1:* 115
Second front
   A *2:* 210–12, 252, 277
Secret agents
   A *1:* 74, *2:* 345–59
Secret code
   B 175–79
Secret police, German
   A *1:* 31, 134, 163, *2:* 349
Secret police, Japanese
   A *2:* 352
Secret police, Russian
   A *1:* 151, *2:* 219
Secret societies (Japanese)
   A *1:* 30–31
Segregation
   B 44, 79
Segregation in the military
   A *1:* 113–17, 114 (ill.)
   B 45, 47–48, 51, 53, 58, 69,
      116, 243, 286
   P 91, 94, 169
Seine
   A *2:* 271

Selective Service Act (draft)
A *1:* 114
Sender, Ruth Minsky
P 101–16
Serbia
A *1:* 74, 154
Sergeant York
A *2:* 380, 380 (ill.)
Service de Travaille Obligatoire
(compulsory labor service)
A *1:* 139, *2:* 242
761st Tank Battalion
A *1:* 115
B 46
Seventh Army (U.S.)
A *2:* 299
7th Panzer (Tank) Division
B 225
Seventh Symphony
(Shostakovitch)
A *2:* 377
Shanghai
A *1:* 32
Sherman tanks
A *2:* 228
Shikai, Yuan
B 18
Shinto Religion
B 94
Ships for Victory
A *1:* 121
Ships, merchant (Japanese)
A *2:* 334
Ships, production of
A *1:* 106
Shostakovitch, Dmitri
A *2:* 377
Shurr, Agnes
P 161–62
Shutzstaffel (*See* SS)
Sicherheitsdienst (*See* SD)
Sicily, Allied invasion of
A *2:* 211, 233–38, 346
B 30, 48,163, 173, 199, 209,
228, 242
P 144
Siegfried Line
A *2:* 291
Signal Corps, U.S. Army
A *2:* 379
B 4
Sikorski, Wladyslaw
A *2:* 218 (ill.), 283 (ill.)

*Since You Went Away: World War II
Letters from American Women
on the Home Front*
P 74–81
Singapore
A *1:* 99
Sino-Japanese War (1895–95)
A *1:* 28, 32
Sit-down strikes
A *1:* 105
Sixth Army (German)
A *2:* 244–46
Skorzeny, Otto
A *2:* 235
Slave Labor
A *1:* 123, 124, 165–66
Sledge, E. B.
P 197–209, 206 (ill.)
Slovak National Rising.
A *1:* 145
Slovakia
A *1:* 23, 41, 144, *2:* 226, 403
Slovenians
A *1:* 154
Sobibór death camp
A *1:* 174
Social Democrats (Germany)
A *1:* 7, 14, 17
Socialism
B 168
SOE (*See* Special Operation
Executive)
Sofia
A *2:* 299
Solomon Islands
A *2:* 314, 317, 317 (ill.)
P 66
Somalia
A *1:* 69
Somaliland
A *1:* 69
Somme River
A *1:* 50
Song of Russia
A *2:* 384
Soong, Mei-Ling
B 19–20
Sorge, Richard
A *2:* 350–51, 351 (ill.)
South Africa
A *1:* 61
Southeast Asia
B 160, 161

South-Eastern Europe
  A *2:* 297 (ill.), 298
Soviet Army
  A *1:* 43, *2:* 268
Soveit Army, women in
  A *1:* 196–97, 197 (ill.)
Soviet Union
  A *1:* 36, 37, 65, 77–82, 79 (ill.),
    2: 216, 218, 222, 223, 248,
    252, 384, 394
  B 30
Soviet Union, American
    Lend-Lease aid to
  A *1:* 65
Soviet Union, German invasion
    of
  A *1:* 77–82, 79 (ill.)
  B 242, 251–54, 266
Soviet Union, Katyn massacre
  A *2:* 218
Soviet Union, losses during
    the war
  A *2:* 392
Soviet Union, partisans
  A *1:* 149–52, 151 (ill.), 196–97,
    196 (ill.)
Soviet Union, relations with
    Allies
  A *2:*206–07, 212, 215–22
Soviet Union, relations with
    Japan
  A *1:* 29, 87, *2:* 220–22,
    332–33, 339
Soviet Union, war with Germany
  A *1:* 77–82, *2:* 278–82, 281
    (ill.), 295–97, 301–04
Soviet-Japanese Neutrality Treaty
    (1941)
  A *1:* 87, *2:*220
Soviet-Polish relations
  A *2:* 282
Spanish Civil War
  A *1:* 13, 21, *2:* 224
Spanish-American War
  B 54
Special Operations Executive
    (SOE)–British
  A *1:* 155, *2:* 353–55
Spies
  A *2:* 349–56
  (*See also* Intelligence)
Sri Lanka (*See* Ceylon)

SS
  A *1:* 148, 160, 164–65, 166,
    176, 179
  B 86, 87, 108, 126
  P 112, 114
St. Petersburg (*See* Leningrad)
St.-Lô
  A *2:* 269
Stalcup, Ann
  A *1:* 202
Stalin, Joseph
  A *1:* 37, 151, *2:* 213, 217, 220,
    221 (ill.), 223, 245, 285,
    336 (ill.), 351, 384
  B 245–55, 31, 245 (ill.), 250
    (ill.)
  P 10, 33, 38–39, 39 (ill.), 119,
    120, 123, 140
Stalingrad, Battle of
  A *2:* 244–46, 246 (ill.)
  P 37, 39
Stalingrad, Battle of, women in
  A *1:* 197
Stanley, Jerry
  P 85–95
Staple Inn, London
  A *1:* 182 (ill.)
Star and Stripes (U.S. Army
    newspaper)
  A *2:* 389
Starvation
  A *1:*136, *2:* 394
Stauffenberg, Count Claus von
  A *2:* 288–89
Stein, Edith
  B 256–62, 256 (ill.)
Steinbeck, John
  A *2:* 383
Stewart, James
  B 4
Stilwell, General Joseph W.
  B 22
Stimson, Henry
  A *1:* 114
  B 152, 191
STO (*See* Service de Travaille
    Obligatoire)
Storm Troopers
  A *1:* 10, 11 (ill.), 158, 160
  B 84, 103, 267
The Story of G.I. Joe
  A *2:* 390
  B 210

The Story of the Malakand Field Force
   B 26
Strategic air offensive
   A *1:*189, 193
Strategic bombing
   A *1:* 183–94, *2:* 334
Strikes
   A *1:* 105, 112, 142–43
Sturmabteilung (*See* Storm Troopers)
Submarines
   A *1:* 45, 66–69, 68 (ill.),
      2: 333–34, 355
   P 43–58, 52 (ill.), 61
Subways (London) as bomb
      shelters
   A *1:* 185 (ill.), 200
Sudan
   A *1:* 69
Sudetenland
   A *1:* 21, *2:* 402, 404
   P 31, 102
Suez Canal
   A *1:* 69
Suffrage movement
   B 217, 264
Suicide, Japanese soldiers on Attu
   A *2:* 316
Suicide, kamakazi pilots
   A *2:* 325, 329, 331–32
Sun Yat-Sen
   B 18, 19
Supreme Court (U.S.), and
      Japanese Americans
   A *1:* 129
Supreme Headquarters Allied
      Expeditionary Forces in
      Europe (SHAEF)
   B 77
Suribachi, Mount
   P 145, 145 (ill.)
Surrender, German
   A *2:* 304
   P 214–15
Surrender, Japanese
   A *2:* 339–40, 343 (ill.), 344
   B 97, 143, 190, 276, 285
   P 215–20, 215 (ill.), 216 (ill.)
Sweden
   A *1:* 45–47, 46 (ill.)
Switzerland
   A *1:* 138, *2:* 354

Sword Beach (D-Day)
   A *2:* 260, 260 (ill.), 264–65
   P 174
Synagogues
   A *1:* 160, 164
Szilard, Leo
   A *2:* 366
   P 126

T

Taiwan
   A *1:* 28, *2:* 411
Tanks, production of
   A *1:* 106
Tarawa
   A *2:* 319
Tasaka, Hiroko
   P 133–36, 138, 139
Teenagers
   A *1:* 121
Teheran Conference
      (November 1943)
   A *2:* 217
   P 221
Televaag
   A *1:* 141
Teller, Robert
   B 191
Teresa Benedicta of the Cross
      (*See* Stein, Edith)
Terkel, Studs
   A *1:* 108
Thames River, bombing of
      docks on
   A *1:* 57, 186
"Their Finest Hour"
   P 13–17
Third Army (U.S.)
   A *2:* 269, 298
Third Reich
   B 107, 123
Thirty Seconds Over Tokyo
   A *2:* 385
Thompson, Dorothy
   B 263–71, 263 (ill.)
369th Cavalry New York
      National Guard
   B 57
332nd Fighter Squadron
   B 49
Tibbets, Lieutenant Colonel
      Paul W.
   P 131, 131 (ill.)

Tinian
  A *2:* 320
Tiso, Father Josef
  A *1:* 145
Tito, Josip Broz
  A *1:* 155–56
To Hell and Back
  B 5
To Life
  P 109
Tojo, Hideki
  A *1:* 88, 88 (ill.)
  B 96, 97,**272–77**, 272 (ill.),
    276 (ill.)
  P 66, 67 (ill.)
Tokyo, American bombing of
    (March 1945)
  A *2:* 335
Tokyo, bombing of by Doolittle
  A *1:* 101
Tokyo (Edo) Bay
  A *1:* 25
Tokyo Express (Guadalcanal)
  A *2:* 315
Tokyo Rose (Iva Toguri Ikoku)
  A *2:* 373
Tolstoy, Leo
  A *2:* 377
Tomara, Sonia
  A *2:* 387
Topp, Erich
  P 55
Torch, Operation
  A *2:* 228
Total war
  A *1:* 181–204
Toulon, French fleet at
  A *2:* 232
Transports to death camps
  A *1:* 174, 174 (ill.)
Treaty of Versailles
  A *1:* 4, 19
  B 108, 224
Treblinka death camp
  A *1:* 174
Tregaskis, Richard
  A *2:* 385
Tripartite Pact
  A *1:* 86 (ill.), 87, *2:* 225–26
  B 241, 274
  P 17, 28, 61
Triumph des Willens (See *Triumph
    of the Will*)

Triumph of the Will
  A *2:* 374
Trotsky, Leon
  B 249
Truman Doctrine
  B 285
  P 123
Truman, Harry S.
  A *2:* 223, 336 (ill.), 341
  B **278–88**, 51, 144, 145, 154,
    190, 214, 244, 278 (ill.),
    284 (ill.)
  P **117–28**, 118 (ill.), 140,
    211–22
Tube Alloys (British atomic bomb
    project)
  A *2:* 365
Tunisia
  A *2:* 229, 231
Turkey
  A *1:* 4
Tuskegee Airmen
  A *1:* 117
  B 43, 47–48, 50, 51
  P 91
Tuskegee Institute
  B 44, 56, 57
20th Century-Fox
  A *2:* 380, 381

U

U-boats (*See* Submarines)
Ukraine
  A *1:* 76, 78, 151, 171, *2:* 248
Ukraine, collaboration with
    Germans in
  A *1:* 151
Ultra
  A *2:* 358, 359
Unconditional surrender
  A *2:* 216, 335
Underground, Polish
  A *2:* 282
  (*See also* resistance)
Unemployment (Germany)
  A *1:* 10
Union of Soviet Socialist
    Republics (*See* Soviet Union)
Unions
  A *1:* 105, 108, 112
United Kingdom
  P 175 (map)

United Nations
  A *2:* 409 (ill.), 409–10
  B 241, 282
  P 23, 214, 221
United States, aid to other
    countries
  A *1:* 63, 84, *2:* 240, 248, 404
    (*See also* Lend-Lease Act)
United States, and relations
    with Britain
  A *2:* 207
United States, and relations
    with the Soviet Union
  A *2:* 221, 342
United States, anti-Nazi
    feelings in
  A *1:* 63
United States, economic
    conditions, 1945
  A *2:* 403, 405
United States, enters World War I
  A *1:* 4
United States Holocaust
    Memorial Museum
    (USHMM)
  P 114
United States, homefront
  A *1:* 105-29
United States, isolationism in
  A *1:* 62
United States, joint defense
    planning with Canada
  A *1:* 65
United States, peacetime draft
    introduced
  A *1:* 65
United States, pro-Allied
    feelings in
  A *1:* 61
United States, reaction to Nazi
    anti-Semitism in
  A *1:* 63
United States, rejects of Treaty of
    Versailles
  A *1:* 6
United States, relations with
    Japan
  A *1:* 25, 31, 86, 88, 96
United States Steel Corporation
  A *1:* 107
Unoccupied zone (France)
  A *2:* 232
Uprising, Warsaw (1944)
  A *2:* 283

Uranium-235
  P 118
US Pacific Fleet
  P 61, 64
USS *Arizona*
  A *1:* 90, 92, 92 (ill.), 118
  P 60 (ill.), 61, 67
USS *Bunker Hill*
  A *2:* 331 (ill.)
USS *California*
  A *1:* 90, *2:* 325
USS *Enterprise*
  A *1:* 103
USS *Hornet*
  A *1:* 101, 103
USS *Lexington*
  A *1:* 101, 102 (ill.)
USS *Liscome Bay*
  A *1:* 118
USS *Missouri*
  A *2:* 344
  B 143
  P 214
USS *Nevada*
  P 61
USS *Oklahoma*
  A *1:* 90
USS *Shaw*
  A *1:* 91 (ill.)
USS *West Virginia*
  A *1:* 90, *2:* 325
  P 61, 63 (ill.)
USS *Yorktown*
  A *1:* 101
USSR (*See* Soviet Union)
Ustashi
  A *1:* 154, 156
Utah Beach (D-Day)
  A *2:* 260, 260 (ill.), 265
  P 174

V

V for victory
  A *1:* 48, *2:* 371
  P 10
V-1 (flying bomb)
  A *2:* 353, 360
V-2 (rocket)
  A *2:* 361, 361 (ill), 362
Vallon, Suzanne
  B 70
VE (Victory in Europe) Day
  B 282

Vella Lavella
   A *2:* 318
Verney, Denise
   B 70
Versailles Treaty (*See* Treaty of
      Versailles)
Veterans
   A *2:* 406
Veterans of D-Day
   P 173–86
Vichy France
   A *1:* 85, 146, 148, *2:* 229, 232
   B 65–67
Victor Emmanuel III, King
   A *2:* 235
   B 170
   P 213
"Victory gardens"
   A *1:* 111
   P 81
Victory in the West
   A *2:* 376
"Victory tax"
   P 72
Vienna
   A *2:* 211
Viet Minh
   A *2:* 416
Vietnam
   A *1:* 84, *2:* 416
   B 221
Vilna
   A *1:* 134, *2:* 280
Virginia Military Institute (VMI)
   B 148
Vistula
   A *2:* 280
Vistula River
   A *2:* 295
Vogelkop (New Guinea)
   A *2:* 321
*Voices of D-Day: The Story of the
      Allied Invasion Told By Those
      Who Were There*
   P 177–84
Volga
   A *2:* 244
Volksdeutche (ethnic Germans)
   A *1:* 133
Vom Rath, Ernst
   A *1:* 160
Von Choltitz (*See* Choltitz,
      Dietrich von)

W

WAAC (*See* Women's Auxiliary
      Army Corps)
WAC (*See* Women's Army Corps)
Waffen-SS
   A *1:* 162, *2:* 293
WAFS (*See* Women's Auxiliary
      Ferrying Squadron)
Wagner, Richard
   A *2:* 377
Wainwright, Gen. Jonathan
   A *2:* 344
"Waiting for Tomorrow"
   P 152–54
Wake Island
   A *1:* 95
   P 61, 65
Wake Island (war film)
   A *2:* 385
Wannsee Conference
   A *1:* 171
War bonds
   A *1:* 107–08
   P 72
War correspondents
   A *2:* 385–87, 386 (ill.), 388 (ill.)
War crimes
   A *2:* 400
   (*See also* Nuremberg trials)
War crimes trials (Tokyo)
   A *2:* 410
   (*See also* Nuremberg trials)
War Relocation Authority (WRA)
   P 87, 91
War ships
   A *1:* 27 (ill.)
Warlords (China)
   A *1:* 33
Warner brothers
   A *2:* 381
Warner, Jack
   A *2:* 384
Warsaw
   A *1:* 24, 166, 182, *2:* 280, 282,
      283, 286, 296
Warsaw ghetto
   A *1:* 167
Warsaw ghetto uprising (1943)
   A *2:* 286
Warsaw uprising (1944)
   A *2:* 219, 285–86
Wasilewska, Wanda
   A *2:* 284 (ill.)

WASPs (*See* Women's Airforce
  Service Pilots)
WAVES (*See* Women's Naval
  Service)
Wayne, John
  B 4
Weinberg, Gerhard L.
  A *2:* 412
Wellman, William
  A *2:* 390
Werner, Herbert A.
  P 43–58
West Germany
  A *2:* 396
West Point
  B 43, 45, 47, 74, 137, 138, 194,
  195
West Virginia, USS (*See* USS *West
  Virginia*)
West wall (or Westwall)
  A *2:* 291
Westermann
  A *1:* 174
Western Allies, and Soviet Union
  A *2:* 206
Western front
  A *2:* 251–75, 278, 291–300
White Russia (Belarus)
  A *1:* 76, *2:* 248, 278, 279,
  280, 282
Why We Fight
  A *2:* 379
  B 6, 7
Willie and Joe cartoons
  A *2:* 389
  B 207
Wilson, Woodrow
  A *1:* 6
  P 24
Winter line (*See* Gustav Line)
Winter position (*See* Gustav Line)
Winter War (1939–40)
  A *2:* 279
With the Marines at Tarawa
  A *2:* 379
*With the Old Breed at Peleliu and
  Okinawa*
  P 199–204
Wloclawek
  A *1:* 164
Wolf packs
  A *1:* 66
  P 45

Woman of the Year
  B 269
Women, in Britain
  A *1:* 122, 197
Women, in Germany
  A *1:* 122
Women, in Japan
  A *1:* 31, 124
Women, in the Soviet Union
  A *1:* 122, 196
Women, in U.S. workforce
  A *1:* 108, 119–20, *2:* 369
  P 72, 72 (ill.), 82, 82 (ill.)
Women in World War II
  A *1:* 196–99, 197 (ill.), 199 (ill.),
  200 (ill.), *2:* 378
  B 38-40, 68, 70, 113–19, 263,
  266, 268, 269
  P 159–69, 160 (ill.), 163 (ill.),
  167 (ill.), 168 (ill.)
Women, war correspondents
  A *2:* 385–86, 386 (ill.)
Women's Airforce Service Pilots
  (WASPs)
  A *1:* 199
  B 34, 40
Women's Army Corps (WAC)
  A *1:* 198
  B 113, 118
Women's Auxiliary Army Corps
  (WAAC)
  A *1:* 198
  B 113, 114, 117, 118
Women's Auxiliary Ferrying
  Squadron (WAFS)
  B 38, 40
Women's Naval Service (WAVES)
  A *1:* 116
Women's Suffrage Movement
  B 216
Women's Voluntary Service
  (WAS) (Britain)
  A *1:* 197
World War I (1914–18)
  A *1:* 3–8, 54, *2:* 252, 391
  B 25, 56, 63, 75, 83, 102, 138,
  149, 158, 169, 195, 218, 224,
  258, 265, 279
  P 6, 14, 21, 35, 122, 156
Wroclaw
  A *2:* 296

Y

Yalta Conference
  A *2:* 221 (ill.)
  B 243
Yamamoto, Admiral Isoroku
  A *2:* 357
  P 61, 68
Yamato (Japanese battleship)
  A *2:* 329
A Yank in the RAF
  A *2:* 380, 381
Year of Decisions (*See Memoirs by
    Harry S. Truman Volume 1:
    Year of Decisions*)
Years of Trial and Hope
  B 288
York, Alvin
  A *2:* 380
Yorktown
  A *1:* 103
Your Job in Germany
  B 8
Yugoslavia
  A *2:*298–99

Yugoslavia, deaths in
  A *2:* 392
Yugoslavia, division of by Axis
  A *1:* 74
Yugoslavia, German invasion of
  A *1:* 73
Yugoslavia, Italian troops in
  A *2:* 236
Yugoslavia, resistance in
  A *1:* 152–56, 153 (ill.)

Z

Zanuck, Darryl F.
  A *2:* 380–81
Zealand
  A *1:* 61
Zhukov, Marshal Georgi K.
  A *1:* 81–82, *2:* 296
  B 252, 253
Zinoviev, Grigori
  B 249
Zoot suit riots
  A *1:* 118

DATE DUE